One 'n Done #8

Wind to Space

sketches & poems by
Rowan Kilduff

Published by

ISBN: 978-1-960869-06-7

LCCN: 2024930493

Mixed Media

Poetry

Climatology

Nature Poetry

For more information on *Wind to Space* or Read Furiously, please visit readfuriously.com. For inquiries, please contact info@readfuriously.com.

Read: [*v*] The act of interpreting and understanding language, symbols, and the written word.

Furiously: [*adv*] To do something with excitement and passion.

Read Often. Read Well.
Read Furiously

Neigh-Bur-Hood Poems

thru words (places, peoples) —
neigh from neah "near" &
bur / (ga)būraz (from bheue- "to be, exist, grow") &
hood, from -had "the position & condition or quality of being," from haidus — literally "bright appearance," from (s) kai- "bright, shining" & ketu "brightness"

Short List

Kestrels & falcons &
Goshawks &   You're
Hawks nest
right in the   a nexus
city limits.
Field mice.   for
About 65 acorns.
Chickadees.   ten thousand
Spruce trees.
Neighbor with her big kaboose!   & more lives
Slovakians
Czechoslovakians (?)   wherein
Vietnamese
The Chinese mechanic   a billion worlds
Streams
Juniper cat   arise
The Mexican woman next door
Stars (Bright Sirius,   (Miracles
The Bear Guardian, Swooping Eagle,   within
The Northern Sky)   miracles)
Planets
Dragonflies   with
Many unknowns   sunrise eyes
(tiny energies)
The grass-roots & air

CO—GROW this brightness
— in the blackberry-2-spruce-mountain-cabin-neighbour-
hood, wolves howl

& hawks
 LOVE

Wife & son sleep holdin' each other & I get up to feed the
wood-stove

S   K   Y   A   B   O   V   E

                                         bless
                               this temporary
                                          home
                                         & all
                                          who
                                          live
                                         in it.

        I listen to their sleeping — Little Bear snoring, a
        soft blow on the embers &
        find my way to bed   by their glo.

3

Hey, how'd ya get so muddy?
Want some hot tea?
Wanna tell me?
Don't wanna tell me
so what you wanna do?
Mami says 'wash yer paws.'

I make some coffee, think on peace

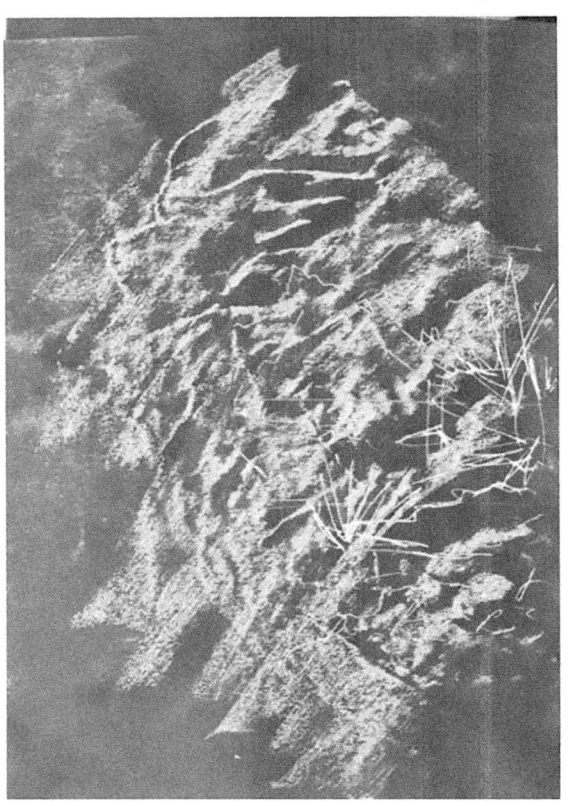

mountain!
— forest!
— wind!

raising up a mountain,
riding with a redtail hawk,
growing with a juniper bush,
sheltered by radiance,
travelling
by night.
A thousand-year old Cedar,
five-thousand year old Bristlecone,
seven-thousand year old Yakisugi,
ten-thousand year Old Tjikko,
sixty-thousand year old Aspens,
millions-of-year old Mountains —
Take a look and celebrate.
Take a look —

shooting star ———
(a halo 'round our feet)
We stay up
cook on the gas stove,
tent rippling.

Thundering
shoreline.
Must be

a basking shark
close-by
travelling

peacefully.
Light-
  skimming-
  waves.

The   source   of   spoken   words,

the   source   of   written   form

The source

   of rivers & wind-form sky-expressions of trail magic & light

W   O   N   D   E   R   M   E   N   T

       is what beats totalitarianism

       Puts an end to the
       war on nature (on my
           nature,
           on yours
               on
               your
            h e a r t)

       (is medicine for bullshit)

Blessed be
this great
continuity

(as a side note, I'll say just this —)

talking to the TRUE,
BOUNDLESS in the wonder-flash
RUNNING for the real
I am still in love.

      whisper — swift wing sings a thunder

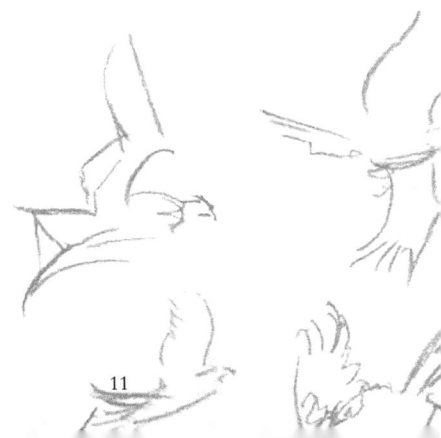

and there it was

— and   s e e i n g   s t a r s — wow

FOR THE BEATIFICATION OF ALL BEINGS IN THIS LIFE & O

no time / space O R

                A   N   Y   T   H   I   N   G

FOR THE UNIVERSAL CITIZENSHIP OF ALL LIFE! sun-dogs,
solar flares, rocks & trees, the air we breathe…

Swifts lift one giant wing over the city (*how do they do that?*)

I don't know much about the great mystery but I think there is
a *clear voice*; flutter of tiny heart of swift
runs thru each life
runs thru
runs thru
& I run thru

THE BRIGHT-TRUE & MIGHTY-NOW where we find a place
make a home

to be FREE ? for who ? d'ya see ?

                         KIDS ARE ONLY FREE AS WE HELP 'EM BE

GREAT DESERT SAGES SPEND TOO MUCH TIME IN THE
DESERT
Peace activist spend too much time
fighting

break the SKY ?

YOU CAN'T BREAK THE SKY

"GONE
GONE
Into the cool
O MAMA!"

running &

Sky cedar

dreaming shadow

(one breath poems)

cabin   friendly   sparks —   fireflies

(after ISSA)

Bright edge —   Mountain &   The Milky Way

(after SHIKI)

I'm still tryin' to catch your tail
               (after / addressed to NANAO)

largerthanlife! sky-encompassing!

a trans-
     lucent
diamond
world
a too-beautiful-to-be-true-and-yet-is
world

     starts right here.

˜What he saw I can't tell ya, but man,
this is the truth about how everything got started…
The wind, and with the waters…
Words for a song ???
& when I find a few words
I fit them in   (as if they were ever adrift!)"

Day by day, day by day and day by day
your sunrise glows, don't matter if no-one knows

Yip-yip-yip-yip-yip-yip — snow & so
many city lights
  make a MIDNIGHT SUN.

2am.
man, these snow-plow guys get up earlier than the Dalai
Lama

the engine runnin' goes

Buddha-Buddha-Buddha-Buddha-Buddha-Buddha-Buddha-

Tungsten lights, twinkling Christmas lights & beyond all
those — a special kind of light all to its own —

                    lil' blackbird song
                    in the icy air.

You're almost 8 yrs old
this year, in place of Christmas, I'd like to give you
a plain real-man Jesus

a world without armies
a new tree planted
an alpine flower in the wind of your imagination

There's nothing he doesn't know — boy stomping snow

CEDARS,

luminescence. The essence

                              talkin' sense

— carving this wood, carving the sun

the light hits my eyes
                         arrive.

from reading p e t e r b l u e c l o u d

– done got his guts busted open on the maple tree, put it
all back in – well he landed butt-first tryin' to fly like a maple
leaf BUT THEY WARNED HIM not no try (you'll break yr ass
they said but he was havin' none of it, and he had no fear of
heights, so that was alright but was not really the point that
the maple-lees were makin') –
c o y o t e walks 'round with p e t e r b l u e c l o u d, and
not a lot of people tellin' these stories anymore; but people
still call G E R O N I M O when they're about to jump off
somethin' and should they die he will guide them to the
d e e p r o c k and s k y (no matter from where they came or
what they believe) – & c o y o t e ?

E V E L K N I E V E L and R O A D R U N N E R ?

c a n   y o u   s h e d   s o m e   l i g h t   o n
t h i s   a l l ?

2 immortals – I heard – are hitchhikin' across the Planet Earth
– last seen somewhere in
Afghanistan – no-one really knows what they're up to or
what's comin' next

in the jay-screechin' flick-of-blue

Journal-Poems
(Dec `21 – Jan `22)

JUST BIG SKY — JUST MOUNTAIN STORM — JUST YOUR
EYES — JUST

****

If the zany folk tale Pom Poko is to be believed, as well
it might, raccoons already live in our cities and look like
people — this is thanks to their shape-shifting abilities (not
as practiced as fox who have infiltrated all the way up, but
they do their best) — and we don't even notice them —
they go to work, they go to the bar, they watch a lot of
tv, load up on energy drinks and from time to time, meet
together out in a meadow by what's left of the forests —
sing & dance & play — raccoons again — that's how they
get by — they keep stories & songs alive and give honors
due & listen to the oldest grandma & grandpa raccoons —
old bushy tails & gnarly-butts — they get all the youngsters
together and freely share all they know 'bout how to live
— "treat your mama with respect" & things like that — what
about all the other animals? Where are they hiding out, if
anywhere? Well, way I see it is they all live right alongside
us & even jay (loud as he is) keeps a low profile — under
roadside bushes, on top of the antenna and in hope spots
here & there the real spirit animals throw a party and keep
us company thru the night — they sometimes take the form
you'd least expect — they will always surprise us
Feels we've been given a second chance

****

I'm 75! Yep, daughter's an astrophysicist in Chile —imagine that! The mountains there are really clear — I take care of the spring, I'll show you the spring if you've got time? -6 All year — still log the forest here, use my horse to pull —my friend's got a heart problem still works the forest — what else is he gonna do? They told him not to work but I've got his Husqvarna up at my place. I'm worried about Afghanistan, saw it on the TV, bad what's happenin' out there — and we have too many refugees (but I'm not from here either, I say.) We need good people 'round here, like you, yeah, you're OK. See you next time you're up this way

****

— All night climbin' to see sunrise — at the top most people sleepin' in sleepin' bags and missed it — clouds at dawn and gentle glory sunrise light
****

(MY FRIEND THE FREE DIVER) SHE LETS HER BREASTS FREE — REACHES FOR THE WINE

****

IT
CREATES A HALO
AROUND A STARBURST
AT THE CENTER OF YOUR IMAGINATION
BLOSSOMS WHIRL
YOUR LIPS PART TO SAY

****

At night a bear came right up to the cottage — right to the compost — at night — in the rain — soft rain — bear came — and I listened — at night — in the rain — soft rain.

****

FOR BEAR —

                    DON'T WRECK HIS
            BLUEBERRIES

In the jeep with a forest ranger and he said to me just like this, straight he said — there's no money in a healthy forest — what are you supposed to say to that? Doing really punk DIY conservation work — hedgehog talkin' to a forest ranger; long hair and beard like one of the Kon Tiki crew, the ranger's saying — get outta here! Hedgehog's sayin' — we belong here (speaks softly, stands butt-naked)

****

AS SOON AS YOU CROSS THAT LINE INTO THE OLD-GROWTH FOREST IT'S THE REAL FOREST — IT'S CRAZY WILD AND WISE AND FREE-TEACHIN' TO ALL THAT WANT TO LISTEN

— WHAT DOES IT SAY? WELL, YOU GOTTA GO THERE, NOTHIN' I CAN SAY ABOUT THAT

Old-growth neighborhood of spruce and fir up there on the snow-covered mountain — that's where you find bear scat and lynx fur and not only that, so much more I don't know where to start — up early, no footprints. And you can see a chickadee in deep winter mornin' go from branch to branch not staying long any place, and you run on by splash in a half-frozen creek dream and rub your hands dry in snow and a hawk cry signals your waking

— EVER-WAKING-NEW

IN AN OLD-GROWTH FOREST AND YOU'D WIPE OUT YR TRACKS IF YOU COULD, MAYBE FLY OVER IT

— MAYBE DON'T GO THERE AT ALL

— Young, old-growth forest where a 4x4 can't go and where millions of years, numberless brothers & sisters go on happy without you — breath of the sky channeling down and mountains breathing, dreaming and 2 deer ripped to bits, chewed up off the trail sets year skin a-tingling — ripp'd spruce bark, fresh resin and the sun goes way down, further than it can, deep into yr heart — but you know, really there are no words for all that

DO YOU FEEL AT HOME IN AN OLD-GROWTH FOREST? DO YOU FEEL AT HOME WHEN THE SUN GOES WAY DOWN? NIGHT COMES AND YOU STAY OUT THERE FREEZING YR BALLS AND ICE ON YR BEARD BY THE TIME MORNIN' COMES ANEW

Tight vertical grain — the best wood to use, up in the mountain sanctuaries (I'm the son of a carpenter, and love the smell, the feel — covered in sawdust, it's one of the best things) logging truck after logging truck on their way out, trains full and long on the way. And I go to feel

****

THERE ARE A FEW REAL PLACES ON THIS EARTH.
SHERPAS — GLACIER MELT — CHIR PINE & BLUE SPRUCE

— HEATING THE KITCHEN, ALL CROWDED IN TONIGHT

— KIDS' HORIZONS — THE WORLD IS TOO FAR AWAY
— HOSPITAL TOO FAR AWAY — COCA COLA ALWAYS
AVAILABLE

— TOO MANY PEOPLE — TOO MANY TENTS
— TOO MANY MOUNTAINS TO CLIMB

— There goes another coconut crunch wrapper in the wind
to the pure land — to the river of the mother of god — the
river that unites — the river that hopes — she who saves

— the continuous waking of clear sight — THE INFINITE
LAYERS TO THE SKY — let the river live / let the people live
— part of ourselves, the Suomi say — 'part of ourselves' is
just the start of it — (and they were scared to put Arne Næss
in jail for defending the river back in the 70's)

— In any case, when a man must be afraid to drink freely
from his country's rivers and streams that country is no
longer fit to live in. Time then to move on, find or make
a new country — "a wilder-ness forever future" — peaks
higher than our consciousness can reach and with melted
down washed away river lifelines

— Fr. Ignacio Ellacuría said what the 'discoverers' did was
not descrubrimento (discovery) but encrubrimento (cover-
up) — the US blew him away

— JUST: A FLASH! — PEACE SIGN, PEACE ON T-SHIRTS —
SHE'S GOT A LOVE HEART ABOVE HER LEFT ELBOW, THE
NUCLEAR DISARMAMENT SYMBOL OVER HER RIGHT

— THERMONUCLEAR TESTS CONTINUE

— WAVES ROLL

— LOOKIN' STRAIGHT UP IN THE NIGHT SKY THAT'S
WHERE WE'RE MOVIN' TO

WALKABOUT SONG

WHAT'S THE WAY TO PEACE? WALKING ALL THESE WAYS
IN PEACE — WALKING IN BRIGHTNESS — IN THE CRACK-
DAZZLE-SUMMER — MIRROR HAWK — MOUNTAINS AT
THE BREAK OF DAY — SAY, SAY — WHERE IS THE WAY?
THE ZING! OF NOT SEARCHIN' ANYTHING — PEACE
SONGS LIKE SKY — OUT BEYOND THE EDGE OF THE
WORLD — THE RIVER, THE RIVER OF ANCESTORS
WAKING INTO THE FUTURE — THE KIDS SING — THE
KIDS RUN — THE KIDS PLAY — THE KIDS GO HAND-IN-
HAND — DEWY GRASS LIGHT — WATCHIN' LIGHTNING
PLAY IN SILENCE FAR AWAY FROM THE MOUNTAIN-TOP
— WIND PLAY — WONDER OF A WHOOSH OF WIND
THRU TREES, THRU LONG GRASS, THRU A DREAM — THE
WIND BLOWS THRU A DREAM — A PART-REMEMBERED
SPARK — WALKING, WALKING 'I AM A SONG, I WALK
HERE' — EVER RUNNING STREAMS — BORN OF/WITH
THIS EARTH — I FEEL A WAKING SOUND — I FEEL
THE EARTH SOUND — I HEAR A WAKING — I HEAR
A-WAKING SOUND — I FEEL THE EARTH SOUND —
WHOOSH THRU A DREAM — PEACE IS THE RIVER — THE
BRIGHT SILENCE OF THE SUN

MY BROTHER SONG

MY BROTHER , MY BROTHER WHERE HAVE YOU GONE?
SKY ASKS AND WONDERS WHERE HAVE YOU GONE?
FIRST FORESTS SING —
THIS WIND-BORN WORLD WHISPERS — THIS QUICK-
BURNING FLAME — THIS HAPPY-GO-LUCKY LOVE-HEART-
BEATING — QUICK-BEATING — FLEET-FOOTED SONG
WHERE HAS HE GONE?

FORWARD TO NEW YEAR — NEW YEAR SPARKLERS

— TO DRAW WITH FIRE — & LAUGH WITH LIGHT

— SHE BACKLIT BY FIREWORKS

— Lifetimes learnin' just how to love / live
Now peeling ginger & heating up the pan — it's gonna be
buttered ginger carrots — think of how in Korea people
usedta eat so many mandarins in winter their hands were
orange — & new year on the beach in snow up all night
tryin' to keep warm

— All together — a kid dances to hip-hop on a balcony
across from me — shouts 'happy new year!' — A neighbor
waves — he clicks a lighter on, and sings — my son already
sleeps — a pretty girl walks alone — the animals all go hide
from the fireworks — I think of friends — think on new days
— new year sparklers — lit a whole bunch at once — flared
up fast & bright for an instant — John Brandi's got this new
year's poem where he visits Issa — just found it now — I go
build a tipi for Nanao under the stars — all the talks we'd
have! — With the flashing-booming celebration sky I think of
war-torn countries — I listen to the wind light

— I LISTEN TO THE WIND LIGHT — IT'S TRUE THERE'S
NO SPECIAL TIME — BUT TONIGHT — HOLD YOU CLOSE
— BRIGHT FOR AN INSTANT

JAN 1ST — WE PET STINGRAYS — WE DRIVE FOR A FEW
HOURS LISTENIN' SONGS — TOGETHER

****

Beat of raven's wings overhead
The forest is sunset the sunset is raven wing. The
WHH-O—WHH-O—WHH-O—WHH-O—WHH-O—
GETS LOUDER & CLEARER &
FAINTER &
FADES.

****

YOU ARE MANY WOMEN AT ONCE / SPEAKING IN
THUNDERBOLTS — JOHN BRANDI

A kind of Czech version of the Lady of Guadalupe with
lightning bolts on her dress instead of stars, shooting down
zig-zag in arrow-heads near rocky grassy outcrop where first
hunters here hunted long long ago and killed off the wild
animal spirits that kept this place sacred to the real — rain
coming in, rain will wash away all tracks and trespasses thru
the wild heart — the sky will clear it all away — bodhisattva
of compassion / sky woman crashing down — she falls
asleep on my shoulder — she transforms into a river, an
avalanche, a rainbow — she changes the world in a single
glance!

Who are you? Asked Turtle Jack, back from a thousand-year sleep — Are you a Goddess?

Yes, she said 'I'm Goddess. I'm Woman. I'm Miss Universe. I'm Spring Princess. I'm your Sweetheart'

— AND HE KNEW HER THEN — HE KNEW HER THEN —

The planet song will continue long — and we'll join up with that star-burst — we will come again into knowing the pure night — the universe is new — the great ocean universe in one point of light — lovers of lovers and more lovers — and light! Light! Light!

*Turtle Jack/Goddess from Nanao

****

SHE CAME A-WALKIN IN ALL HER MULTI-COLORED BEAUTY — OUT THERE IN
THE FOREST NIGHT — OUT THERE UNDER THE STARS —
I CAME BACK PART SKY

Sweaty eye told me — left in '68 — somersaults at 70, that's what they say —'hey man, i live in the refugee camp you didn't know was here' — the mountains and rivers stay awhile till everything returns — squashed snake on the road, pick it up to have a look — it glints in the sun — the road glints in the sun — rolling waves break the sun into a million & rolls them all into one — thinkin' on Jacques Cousteau —

thinkin' on Nanao chanting for bristlecone pines —
Feel

This is all more real than what's ever in my mind!
'What's this future that's so wonderful? Bunch of folks lovin'
each other' — Juniper replying — Crazy Horse crying to the
north —
Reading about & looking at Ryōkan's calligraphy in the
bright night first snow (far off perfect) invisible ligatures
connect

— Reading Hawkeye — about him & his one-eyed dog
called Lucky — it's all about the neighborhood.

  — We've known each other all our lives
   & Ain't that somethin' ?
A starlit river — thundering light at the edge of 'we' —
5 Eagles

— In some far off time in the future where universal harmony
is a real thing and all our peace-work has come to somethin'
— Manjushri washes his face in the stream, sees Jesus

(Man, I don't have to wait for some future time to love!)

ALTERNATIVE PRESENT MOMENT

WAR IS ILLEGAL.
ALL NUCLEAR WEAPONS HAVE BEEN SHOT INTO THE
SUN.
WE HAVE CLOSED DOWN THE GLOBAL SUICIDE CLUB.
NEW OLD-GROWTH FORESTS START.
CLEAR RIVERS & AIR GREET YOU EVERY MORNIN.
THERE ARE NO HOMELESS PEOPLE BECAUSE — NO
OWNERSHIP — AND NO OWNERSHIP MEANS WE LIVE
LIKE NOMADS — NO COUNTRY — EVERYWHERE IS
HOME, OUR TERRITORY, OUR RESPONSIBILITY.
WE FREE THE HEART-MIND.
WE HAVE SOLVED THE ENERGY PROBLEM.
WE HAVE TRANSCENDED
VIOLENCE
&
APPROACH
THE
LEVEL
OF
WHALES.

SKY HEART

DRIER & DRIER DESERT — MEXICAN IMMIGRANTS WILL
RUN OUT OF WATER FASTER — 4.1 MILLION REFUGEES
IN SOUTH AMERICA TODAY —SAGUARO CACTI ARE
CHOPPED DOWN & LEFT LIKE THAT IN FORMER SACRED-
PROTECTED LANDS — 43 ENDANGERED SPECIES LIVE
IN SONORA — TRILLIONS ARE SPENT ON MILITARY — 1
PERCENT OF THAT COULD GO TO LIFE & FRIENDSHIP —
THERE IS NO BORDER FOR SKY, HEART OR HOPE

fast clouds move across &
this
S   K   Y

WHY'S IT LIKE THIS? ALL THE OTHERS LOOK LIKE
THEY'RE DOIN' JUST FINE — DON'T HAVE TO TRY TO BE
WHO THEY ARE —
NAVAJOS HAVE A STORY THAT WE PASSED THRU 3
WORLDS TO GET HERE TO WHAT THEY CALL THE
GLITTERING WORLD — MAYBE THEY FIRST SAW IT
UNDER THE STARS —

"HEAVENLY ALARMING FEMALE" / EOS – SHE IS THE DAWN

"Her brother ran a half-skinned pony thru the house and flung shit & mud all over the place"

— And the sun went out — the solar ephemeris was no good & really, the earth-as-ecosystem would've died but for a girl who danced with her tits out and pushed down her skirt and got it all out & you know what? The sun goddess who had gotten so angry peeked out again to see her

— And that's what saved the world back in those times, as they tell it — there are a few versions of the story, this one I got from Gary Snyder in *Mountains And Rivers Without End* — and I'm still wonderin' — this French-Canadian girl — tough talkin' smokin' a cigarette like Karen Allen in Indiana Jones, she pulled me right to her jeans, body dancin' sunlight, love
(and she was sweet)

— How do you save the world? Get free & love & love & love & see the sun in each other & freely honor what we've got &
R e a l i s e

The 1st sun in the sky (t u n e   y o u r   e y e s   t o)

The 2nd sun in the body — in the heart — and everything just about that

JACK LOEFFLER TRANSPORTING A BUDDHA IN THE TRUCK

BUDDHA OF THE ETERNAL HIGHWAY!

****

That they will save and carry—

I don't know if there's an intuition gene or a sensitivity-to-the-flow-of nature gene or an opening to-the-night-sky gene or a sense-of-mystery gene or a scared-potential-without-the-baggage gene — Jack Loeffler

T H I S IS HOW WE STAY — STAY — STAY TRUE

Propane blue flame — went out
My wife shouting for me to come
— It's ok, the pilot lights out, that's all — I'll just light it
again — turned the switch — l e f t (not right, that's what
went wrong last time) — loud thunk — lit a match — wife &
son in the bath — he's got the Star Wars action figures and
she stretches out to dunk her hair, water runs in to cover her
belly, pink nipples underwater — I let go the switch — flame
goes out — do the whole thing over again —

TAKE ME OUT UNDER THE SKY — SO I CAN BE FREE —
TAKE ME OUT UNDER THE SKY —
TO MY GOOD FRIENDS WHEN I DIE:
GIVE ME A SKY BURIAL
(TAKE ME SOMEPLACE IT'S NOT AGAINST THE DAMN
LAW)
SET THE NIGHT ALIGHT
SO I CAN BE FREE — TAKE ME OUT UNDER THE SKY —
WHERE THE VAST STORM CARRIES — THE FIRST LIGHT
OF THE NEW —
TAKE ME OUT UNDER THE SKY —

(this
bright life)
sweet sister, all them hawks and kites shot for no good
reason.
yet, their sunset eyes hold us no hate.

(this
hope)

man runs up hugs his grandma she says
"go on now boy!"

snow-covered pine tree:
teenage embrace
common ground in this polarized neighborhood?
heart space

Wind to Space

w a v e s caused by w i n d caused by s o l a r winds —
s t a r s & all galaxies moved and held together by d a r k
e n e r g y / d a r k g r a v i t y ?— (interaction of a parallel
universe ?) — h i g h e r dimensional space and the
m u l t i v e r s e ? (and this moment's just a c l o u d
of possibilities) — there might be K a l - E l reading comic
books about y o u & me

& w e a l l g l o l i k e c a r o l d a n v e r s
(i m a g i n a t i o n might be b o r d e r t o n o t h i n g)

West to — Where?

naked sky

"Free Goddess of Mercy,"

I chase the light

one,   two,   three,   *infinity*

"Your thighs are appletrees. Your knees are a southern
breeze."

Evrythin's goin' whur it's goin'

Cloud-chief traveling East, passes 'branches of a whirlwind.'
Maybe that was an old tree, a big-old-mythical tree, and he
meets this Old Man who's jumping around LIKE THIS —
He says, "what are you doing?" and the Old Man answers
"I was having fun till now." And he asks him some questions
about life. At first the Old Man hesitates, but then agrees to
answer.

THE SHORT VERSION:

Cloud Chief asks	The Old Man answers
Why is everything messed up?	people think they're In charge
What can I do?	Harass those bastards!
How?	Like a spirit
But how?	738 days in a redwood is really somethin'
Can you give me some instructions?	Don't be one of those

                                        contrary old
                                        sons-of-a-bitches

I don't know, are you really
a wise man?   WOAH
                                        WHADAHELLISTHAT ?!

What?   Ten thousand of those
                                          darndest things
                                          just runnin' all around,
                                          no-one knows why

Where are
you going?   INTO THE DEEP-
                                        boundless blue

Cloud Chief runs after him, meets a deer who says 'brother,
there's a world of things you can do.''

                              (this was based on Chuang Tzu)

He Who Is His Own Sail meets *The Wind Goddess*

(she says "don't hold me too tight")

before she was born
before she was born
before breath born
born before breath

hawk

      brushes
      sky
      &

        sunny
      I frazzy
        hair
        in the wind ——- blow
        in my eyes

color on hand
    on brush

color on t-shirt
     mug
     beard
      &

all i n d i g o
all r a i n b o w

       yr
   " raw sienna " feet

(Forest,   amber   color over

     - glide,   yr head)

          cerulean
          woman

                                    THIS PLAIN
                                    UNIVERSE
                              is gnarly,   is kind

I go to my woman
                  wanna press you
                to   my   body   & roll around in yr

                                        easy grace.

Tangerine,
at age 22 was the girl who did the ''*Who's afraid of
Ai Weiwei?*'' graffiti

      Hers was a peace protest
         where's ''peace'' at?
(It's in the Uyghur Nation! Navajo Nation!)
                              - *Who's afraid of freedom?*
      hope
      we send

Because ''if you don't speak out
and you don't clear your mind
then, who are you?''

How about one borderless world
         of kin / kindness?
         make art / make possibilities

         ''Love the Future''

Heart-lit – totally Heart-lit

going toward RAINBOW
mind: a planetarium ——————————
silver-lining
of the body
(family — BIG EARTH family)

There's a wildfire story about a dove who tried to put out
the fire but died and opened up her buddhafield (THE
BUDDHAVERSE) — she GOT BORN
— fighting against what's "impossible" was the key thing
but the ke-yest thing was not fighting; LOVIN' this world
exactly as it is
PEACE! PEACE! PEACE! PEACE!   FIRE IN MY BELLY!
HEY NOBLE ONE here is a field of possibilities —
no things or countries or
HEAT
The earth is polluted - the water is polluted - the air is
polluted
only FIRE burns clean
(how many before armies disappear? countries?)
JESUS — 2 syllables, easy
AVALO-KITE-SHVARA

She's healing waters w / BLUE MEDICINE
YOUTH with love burning inside
GENTLE youth
need hands and tools and hands are made for tools and
kindness, open hands, giving life hands, universal-peace
hands, hands reaching out to yr hands
       if we were made for somethin else we'd have
VELOCIRAPTOR hands or armor-plated hands — but we got
these flexible miracle things to make / break

to put out fires

EARTH DISSOLVES INTO WATER   mirages
WATER TO FIRE   smoke
FIRE TO WIND   rush of fireflies

— WIND TO SPACE —————

                              COOL LIGHT
                              —————

                                ————

                                ———

                              SUN LIGHT
                              —————

                                ————

                                ———

                              DARK SKY

                                ————

                                ———

                              PRE-DAWN
                              (deep in the chest)

Author's notes:

13 - "gone gone…" from Philip Whalen's take on the Heart Sutra, in the book *On Bear's Head*.

20 - "cedar shadow" — Peter Blue Cloud

30 - "move on, find or make a new country" — Ed Abbey

30 - "a wilder-ness forever future" — Howard Zahniser via Doug Scott

32 - "I am a song, I walk here" (from the Hopi); "The bright silence of the sun" — said by Nanao Sakaki (recorded by Will Staple; in *Nanao or Never*, Blackberry Books.)

37 - "what's this future that's so wonderful? …" — Jeff Bridges, Rolling Stone

37 - Hawkeye, 2012 Marvel Comics.

43 "that they will save and carry" — Jack Loeffler's *Headed Into the Wind*

50 - WIND TO SPACE — This is a Buddhist mediation process, and can be read as that. I got it from Bob Thurman. "Heart-lit totally heart-lit" is largely me writing things down while listening to his talks.

53 - "one, two, three, infinity" the title of a book by Gadow/ basic idea of the shinto prayer /popular buddhist theme (Ryōkan's 1, 2, 3); "appletrees" quote is from William Carlos Williams

55 - Julia "Butterfly" Hill spent 738 days in a thousand yr old California redwood.

61 - Tangerine is an artist-activist from Hong Kong. "Love the Future" is a play on Ai Weiwei's name.

64 - "blue medicine" — the blue Medicine Buddha: blue because of the sky; the space element.

/ can be read as 'or', or an unvoiced 'or', a pause.

Walkabout Song first appeared in a DIY zebook called *Nanao*, shared among friends on Jan. 1st 2023 (nanaoglobal.com); "Running Sky / Cedar..." & 2 "one breath poems" appear in Fire songs, skysongs, mountain songs; part of "Alternative Present Moment" is on the Greenpeace wall of change (greenpeace.org.uk)

sketches:

Front cover - Solid / Flowing / A New Direction 11.8"x 23.6". Apr. 7 '22 (detail)
chapter title, 2 - swallow at nest, juniper cat
6 - mountain, chalk Apr. '23
7, 10, 16pgs - "hawk in flight" sketches, summer '23+ print...
17 - blue lines for peace (2), Mar. '22
29, 37 - bristlecone pine, tempera & chalk 10 x 8; Machapuchare
21, 28, 30, 38, 48 - trees; godzilla; coyote; whale
30 - Wind-talk acrylic & pencil on paper, from sketchbook. First printed in *The Fourth River*, Pittsburgh & in *Rewilding Earth*.
42 - Jack Loeffler photo & freebird
43 - blue lines for peace (6) tempera on 18" x 12" board, 9.6" x 9.6"Apr. '22

About the Author

photo: Danusia Trzcińska

Rowan Kilduf is also the author of *Fire songs, sky songs, mountain songs; Sunrise Fire*; and his writing & art appears in *Rewilding Earth, Wingspan, Camas, Gulf Stream Magazine, Ecozon@ España*, and in the mini Anthology of American Poets in Italy from *Zest Letteratura Sostenibile* (honorarily). He lives in Central Europe, currently up and down between 49 and 52°N, near what's called the Alpide Belt where hawks fly and mountain ridges go on & on like a Big Sung painting.

About Wind to Space

This book is in a few parts, there are neighborhood poems about the bigger neighborhood of lifeforms, including eventually the whole planet; "one breath poems" which are after Issa, Shiki, poet Nanao Sakaki; journal poems which are without much formatting and can be read in any way; and wind to space poems.

"Wind to Space" comes from a Buddhist meditation but also feels to me as an opening-up of possibilities, getting through separateness; the idea of being here in this place/space where it's all happening.

The sketches were done in a spontaneous way, like most of the poems here. Without much correction once they're put down, to try to go for a decisiveness of energy, a physical move in the world.

Rowan Kilduff
Jan. 2024, BB.

A Note to our Furious Readers

From all of us at Read Furiously, we hope you enjoyed our latest installment in our One 'n Done series, *Wind to Space: poems & sketches*.

There are countless narratives in this world and we would like to share as many of them as possible with our Furious Readers.

It is with this in mind that we pledge to donate a portion of these book sales to causes that are special to Read Furiously. These causes are chosen with the intent to better the lives of others who are struggling to tell their own stories.

Reading is more than a passive activity – it is the opportunity to play an active role within our world. At Read Furiously, we wish to add an active voice to the world we all share because we believe any growth within the company is aimless if we can't also nurture positive change in our local and global communities. The causes we support are culturally and socially conscious to encourage a sense of civic responsibility associated with the act of reading. Each cause has been researched thoroughly, discussed openly, and voted upon carefully by our team of Read Furiously editors.

To find out more about who, what, why, and where Read Furiously lends its support, please visit our website at readfuriously.com/our-causes

Happy reading and giving, Furious Readers!

Read Often, Read Well,
Read Furiously!

More in the One 'n Done Series

What About Tuesday
Adam Wilson
978-0-9965227-9-3

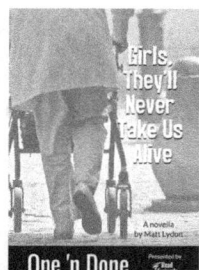

*Gurls, They'll Never Take
Us Alive*
Matt Lydon
978-1-7337360-3-9

Brethren Hollow
Bill Hemmig
978-1-7337360-8-4

Helium
Adam Wilson
and Jeff Chin
978-1-7337360-5-3

*The Legend of Dave
Bradley*
S Atzeni
978-1-7371758-8-9

The Path Home
A.J. Pelligrino
979-8-9868097-8-6